12-2-97

Debie Chris
a friend of mine wrote
This book. It has some
Great stuff in it Grab
some
w/Love
Ugne

Gaining
Essential
Perspectives

by
Jerry Harte

D0068009

PROCTOR PUBLICATIONS, L.L.C., of ANN ARBOR, MICHIGAN

Library of Congress Catalog Card Number: 95-69545

ISBN: 1-882792-13-0

Printed in the United States of America

All is perspective.
The earthworm finds it more relaxing
to dig holes in the ground,
than it is to go fishing.

— Clyde Abel

TABLE OF CONTENTS

INTRODUCTION

Greetings, friends.

This is my opportunity to express my appreciation to you for choosing this book. In reading it, you will in effect, be granting me access to your thought processes. This is a big responsibility which both humbles and inspires me. I will do my best to live up to your expectations.

As you may have already gathered, I prefer writing in a style similar to the way that I speak — casual, forthright, and economically (Okay, the economic part needs some work). It is my desire that reading the words on these pages feels like a conversation. The word "conversation" implies two or more participants in a communication. While it is difficult for books to be truly interactive, your level of participation will determine the success of this communication.

I believe there is a huge and important difference between active and passive reading. I also believe it is one of the responsibilities of a writer to try to stimulate the reader's intellectual activity. For the active reader, words induce thoughts, thoughts induce feelings; thoughts and feelings define the nature of our actions.

When we look back on the impact a book may or may not have had on us, we recall the induced thoughts and feelings that resulted from reading that book. No induced thoughts — no induced feelings — no opportunity for change — no benefit from the book. To me, it's that simple.

It is my greatest wish that you enjoy and benefit from your end of this conversation as much as I have enjoyed and benefited from preparing my part.

ACKNOWLEDGMENTS

Undoubtedly, the person with the second most time, energy, and effort in this text is Rhonda Westfall. Her exceptional patience, insight and editorial skills were instrumental. She also is probably number one on the list of most-relieved that we've finally put this project to bed. Many thanks, Rhonda.

Much of the early transcription of these words was ably handled by a very nice lady named Joann Miller. Also, I sent a number of sample chapters to friends for their critical review, but only Joyce Caulkins took the request seriously. She scrutinized every word and made some enlightening and helpful suggestions, which contributed greatly to the final product.

There are numerous colleagues who have lent their support and helped me immensely. Jack Canfield's warmth, kindness, and insight have aided me more than he will ever know. Same goes for Dr. Bowen White, Bruce Boguski, Leslie Charles, Tom Borg, and Patti Holmes. They energize and lift my spirits every time we speak.

Bob Thompson has been a good client and friend who provides a constant challenge to keep me learning, and moving forward. Tom Woodward has been a benevolent mentor throughout both my good times and bad. The unwavering faith I have felt from these two men has been a beacon. I'll be eternally grateful to both.

Most of what I've done as an adult (both good and bad) has been with the help of my two best friends, Tom Jones and Clyde Weir. This project was not an exception.

I guess I'm luckier than most. I've had three supportive parents through all my many ups and downs. I would be grossly negligent if I did not mention my mother, father, and stepfather and thank them profusely. My little sister has had her moments of special contribution, but I'm choosing not to mention her name (because she asked me to). I would also be remiss in not referring to my grandmother, who placed such a high premium on books and instilled feelings in me that I was to accomplish great things in my life.

Were it not for the unshakable faith and support of my loving wife, Diane, I would still be in prison (40 hours a week). She has sacrificed more than anyone should have to in order for me to find my way. I plan on paying her back with big interest for the rest of my days. (You be nice to her, too, if you see her; she's earned it.)

The contributions that all the aforementioned good people have made to my career and to my life often seem to pale by comparison to the joy and inspiration provided by my daughters, Emily and Allison. Every day at some point, it washes over me that they are my primary reason for existence, and I thank God all over again for the blessings of their births.

GENESIS

At the urging of family members and friends who have endured the brunt of the neurotic behavior which was related to writing this (my first) book, I'll include a few thoughts about how this project came about (they thought you might find it interesting).

During my years of work with various groups, I often employed a tactic intended to spur creative thinking, using the phrase, "Let's work on this backwards." Unknowingly, I was employing a philosophy stated by Dr. Steven Covey in his wonderful book, *The Seven Habits of Highly Effective People.* In that book, Covey's second habit is stated as follows, "Begin with the end in mind." He refers to this as his habit concerning creativity.

Although I'm not quite as articulate as Dr. Covey, using this tactic usually gets the group thinking in a different way, and, in that respect, it has been a successful strategy.

Apparently this constant suggestion of mine to work on things backwards has had some sort of subconscious effect on how I have approached my career. Many speakers were authors first. They were dragged (initially) to the podium at the request of people who wanted to hear them speak about their experiences and the ideas in their books. This has not been the case with me.

The creation of this book is a result of my speaking experiences. For some time now, I've made all or part of my living sharing ideas and concepts (hopefully helpful) with other people by word of mouth.

Relatively early in my speaking career, I began getting requests for additional information and additional thoughts. "Do you have a book? Do you have a tape?"

From these requests, I took this "Let's work backwards" idea one step further. I first made an audio tape. The format that I chose in making it involved putting the concepts that I speak about into the form of affirmations — a goal stated in the first person, present tense, as though it has already been attained. (For the purpose of this book, I will refer to these specific affirmations as "perspectives.") I repeated these perspectives in a rhythmic fashion with relaxation music audible in the background — called a voice-over.

Please note: I am indicating that both the words and music are easily audible — there is no subliminal element. This type of tape helps the listener recall the message and reinforces the desired action. The music is simply a memory booster.

When I compiled the perspectives for the tape, I included what I felt were the most vital concepts from my various presentations. I later realized that I rarely (if ever) cover all of the concepts that are meant to be reinforced by the tape in a single lecture. That means the listener has an incomplete base of information and cannot use the tapes effectively.

Now, finally, I'm writing this book, which will explain all the concepts behind the perspectives. The perspectives reinforce the philosophies contained in my speeches. The circle is finally complete.

Hey, begin with the end in mind. I've been doing it for a long time. I can't see any reason to change now.

PROLOGUE

Probably one of the last things we need in this world is another book on the Self-Help (psycho-babble) bookshelves. Yet, like every author who churns out this stuff, I believe I have a fresh approach.

The final, determining factor for much of our health, well-being, success, and happiness comes from our behaviors. I believe we take basic human action (or inaction) too much for granted. My philosophy about human behavior will be demonstrated through the following thoughts.

I often refer to a model that I call the anatomy of a behavior (adapted slightly from Dr. Covey, again). In this model, there are three basic components to every behavior:

1) The knowledge component, which consists of our ability to recognize the need for or the appropriateness of certain activities.

2) The skill component, which measures how well we are performing a certain activity.

3) The attitude component, that is, how much and why we want to do this activity. What is the motivation behind it?

Now, I've gone and done it. I've used the m-word. I am often referred to as a motivational speaker. This generally annoys me. I often respond with, "Let me tell you everything I know about motivation in one sentence: If you want to motivate people, hold them accountable."

While this is a very effective strategy, the downside is that you will only learn how much (or little) motivation a person already has in regard to a certain activity. If we desire to change activity (motivate) we must understand the nature of (or the logic behind) the existing motivation. This is why the attitude component is so crucial.

Knowledge and skill are objective issues. This means we can quantify or put numbers on these things. They can be measured easily, they can be tested. That is where most of the training/teaching takes place; in the arenas of knowledge and skill.

On the other hand, attitude is much more subjective. Subjective loosely means "subject to opinion." When we deal with subjective issues, we're much more likely to get into personal feelings; we lose our objectivity (which is understandable). We find it hard to measure, hard to understand. We find it difficult to induce (and maintain) change.

What I'll be doing in the chapters that follow is expressing thoughts, or concepts, which are meant to induce a certain essential perspective. Perspective is a key component of attitude. Not only will I be dealing with concepts that, if followed, will benefit your life, I will also be trying to give you perspectives to facilitate the proper posturing of the attitude component of the corresponding behavior. (In English, that means, "Get your mind right.")

Using Perspectives is basically just a way to recall the thoughts, theories, and logic behind the perspectives that I'm choosing to share with you. I believe perspectives are a great way to remind us of the much bigger picture behind the thought processes that can lead to desired behavioral changes.

I often refer to perspectives as "mini-mission statements." A good example might be one I've chosen for myself for this year, which is

"Do Less Better." First of all, it's bad grammar, which makes me smile and reminds me not to take myself so seriously. Second, it addresses a major downfall I've suffered during the past year. Simply put, I tried to take on too much and the result was a flurry of activity, very little of which could be judged as excellent. It was almost as though I decided to "Do More Worse." Hey, that wasn't my plan, but you wouldn't know it, based on the outcome.

1995's battle cry enables me to continually prioritize my activity, narrow my focus, and raise the standard for acceptable results. "Do Less Better" sends me a succinct and comprehensive message intended to keep me on the right track.

Please don't lose sight of the fact that attitude alone is never enough. We must always pay the price for acquiring skill and knowledge. All three components must be in balance before true success (and happiness) can evolve.

One final thought before we roll up our sleeves and get to work. You will soon become aware of the many acknowledgments which will be necessary to give proper credit for the original ideas behind many of the perspectives. I have often said that I use few original thoughts of my own for presentations — but, I borrow the very best from the best. I believe the strength of my contribution is the unique combination of and twists I place on numerous "classics" from the self-help bookshelves.

That said, let's get BUSY. (Apologies to Arsenio)

My Day Begins At Five A.M.

I know what you're thinking: "Aren't these Perspectives supposed to reinforce my goals? Getting up at five o'clock in the morning is definitely not one of my goals. What are you talking about here?"

Guess what? Your day *does* begin at 5 a.m. Whether that's when you get out of bed or not might be another story, but your day does begin at 5 a.m. You can choose to spend the initial one, two, or three hours of your day in bed. But I would like you to consider the benefits of what the people who produce the Franklin Day Planner refer to as the "magic three hours," which, they say, begin at 5 a.m.

Before I get in any deeper, please understand that I am not proposing you get a lesser amount of sleep in any 24-hour period. Sleep is an important part of rest and recuperation; I am not a proponent of sleeping less.

Let's say that normally you go to bed at midnight and begin your day at 7 a.m.; that's seven hours of sleep. In order to begin your day at 5 a.m., and still get seven hours of sleep, instead of ending the day at midnight you will have to go to bed at 10 p.m.

Entertain this scenario: Let's say for some reason unknown to you at the present time, you do crawl out of bed at five o'clock in the morning. You take a shower or a bath, eat a good breakfast, and then plan your day. Wouldn't you be bright-eyed, bushy-tailed and ready to start being constructive by six o'clock in the morning? No sweat, right?

What do you think your level of productivity would be from 6 to 8 a.m? Chances are it would be pretty good, wouldn't it?

Conversely, how do you normally spend those two hours from 10 p.m. to midnight? I would wager that a great deal of that time is spent in front of the television, as a veritable ball of fire, no doubt.

I'm suggesting that you simply make a trade-off. You can greatly increase your productivity merely by trading off 5 to 7 a.m., as sleeping time, for 10 p.m. to midnight.

You need only take a moment to consider the difference. The next time you hear someone (particularly yourself) say, "There simply aren't enough hours in the day..." complete the thought by adding, "...the way I am currently using them." Discretion would dictate this should be done quietly, to yourself (unless you are trying to start an argument).

If you accept the challenge of this theory, getting into the habit of beginning your day at 5 a.m. can result in two additional hours of very productive time each day. That's 10 hours a week (Monday through Friday only), 520 hours a year, or 65 eight-hour work days, which is 13 working weeks. Hey, wake up (literally) and smell the calendar. That's a whole quarter of a year. No wonder those early risers are getting all the worms!

Whether you like it or not, the fact is, your day does begin at 5 a.m. How you choose to use those next precious 24 divisions of time is up to you.

> **The early bird gets first crack at worm futures.**

PERSPECTIVE # 2

I Start My Day With Planning
and Solitude

This Perspective is designed to reinforce a commitment that I suggest you make: work on your plan for life; review that plan the first thing in the morning, and do it in a quiet, peaceful place, void of distractions.

I borrowed the specific phraseology, "planning and solitude," from the Franklin Day Planner people. I guess that's appropriate. The first two Perspectives deal with the beginning of your day. Any good plan must begin at the beginning.

Starting your day with planning and solitude should not be confused with making a to-do list. I was a big proponent of that strategy for a number of years. But when your planning consists only of making to-do lists, you run the risk of focusing only on areas or items that need immediate attention. You may lose sight of long-range plans for the week, the month, the quarter, the year, or even longer.

You may also overlook how your planned actions coincide with the values that you have prescribed for yourself. A list of all of your long-range goals and the action steps necessary to achieve them is vitally important; but no more so than a list of the moral and ethical guidelines that you have set for your behavior. Have these reminders in a handy place where you can briefly review them EVERY SINGLE DAY.

Another danger in using to-do lists is that we often include too many items. We are not very realistic about what we can successfully accomplish in any given day. This overload can create frustration and/or anxiety, which in turn will decrease productivity, which will increase frustration and/or anxiety, which will again lower productivity..... (I think you get the picture). Lovely thing we do to ourselves, don't you think?

Of course, one reason why people are so loyal about to-do lists is because it feels good when items are checked off the list. In fact, people who have used to-do lists for a number of years may get compulsive about them. If something is accomplished during a day that wasn't on the list, they might write that item down and then check it off as being completed. Sound familiar?

> **#1 reason given for why many executives don't plan their days: They don't have time.**

I believe that starting your day with planning and solitude is a great way to create a concise working plan for the day. Another part of that commitment is to make sure you follow the action plan that you've created for yourself.

One suggestion I would make is that you put at least one item on your daily activity list that is not urgent, but would be a significant contribution to the accomplishment of one of your long range goals. You may not get to it every time, but it does ensure that long-range goals are kept a little closer to the front burner; allowing them to slide too far away from daily conscious thought is like looking for ways to fail.

Most of this discussion has centered on planning. The second part of our phrase involves solitude: being alone in a nice, quiet environment, making sure that you are very composed, thinking good thoughts about yourself, being confident — that is a great gift to present to yourself on a daily basis.

This special, personal time should not be part of an exercise program. That's not the idea. This is very specific. It may need to be only five or ten minutes, but you need to take that time by and for yourself.

Some people say, "I like to take my last few minutes at work every day and plan the next day when all the issues that I did or didn't address are still fresh in my mind." There's nothing wrong with that. In fact, there's a great deal of merit to reviewing your schedule and checking upcoming events the night before.

But even if you've designed your plan the night before, begin the new day with quiet time for yourself, even if it's only a few minutes. Then, review that plan, thumb back through your long-range goals, recheck your values, and ask yourself some of those important time-management questions like, "Is this the best use I can make of my time today? Does this reflect the values that are true and important for me?"

The start of your day is a perfect time for planning and solitude, so make a commitment. And remember, beware of using only to-do lists. Your planning and solitude will put you in a frame of mind ready to face the day's challenges at your very best.

I Give Thanks and
Count My Blessings Every Day

For me, this is part of a mental health check list. I believe one factor that leads to the toxic mental attitude that is so prevalent in today's world, is a lack of gratitude. Many times we are focused only on the things that we don't have. We're constantly comparing ourselves to the Joneses and we don't think we measure up. This can lead to a great deal of unhappiness.

I make certain that I begin every day by giving thanks for the incredible gifts I have received. Then I like to take inventory of those blessings, those things for which I am grateful.

> **God did not put us on earth to make a living, He put us here to make a difference.**

If we could measure happiness, quantify it by putting a number on it, our happiness index might be a measurement of our MAG — Magnitude of Attitude of Gratitude.

Being in a mental funk or conducting a "pity party" exhibits a complete lack of recognition of the gifts we have been given. At these times, we focus only on the things that we don't have and ask, "Why me? Why haven't I been lucky? Why don't I own a home? Why don't I have a good-paying job? Why was my plant closed?" It is important to steer clear of the "pity party" questions.

When I make my inventory of blessings, I start by thanking God for this incredible gift of life. It's an up-and-down roller coaster ride, to be sure, but what a magical experience. Too often we lose sight of the joy of just being alive. The gift of life can be translated quite literally, and as such, should be appreciated in accord with its tremendous value.

Regardless of the frustration that I allow some family members to cause me from time to time, I also want to thank God for my gene pool; what a unique and incredible recipe. I thank God for my family.

This is also the time when I stop and reflect on my spirituality. I think about all the gifts I've been given and understand they've really come with no strings attached (at least in any form of communication with which I'm familiar). It is completely up to me how I choose to live my life. I'm very grateful for that freedom, and I want to make sure that my actions reflect that gratitude.

It's almost impossible to be in a bad mood and be grateful at the same time. When I start every day by giving thanks, counting my blessings, and making an inventory of things I'm thankful for, I give myself the best possible chance of starting that day with a positive and upbeat attitude.

Somethin' gotcha down? Check out your MAG. Get real. Crank it up to where it rightfully belongs and watch the world change for the better — right in front of your eyes.

> **"It's almost impossible to be grateful and unhappy at the same time."** — J. Harte

I Love, Nurture, and Cherish
My Family

As I list my personal hierarchy of priorities, family always ranks in the top two or three, probably most often number one. Every day I renew the vision of just exactly how important my family is to me. "Family" to me means my own, present nuclear family — my wife, Diane, and our two daughters, Emily and Allison. My family is a key component of my MAG — I want to refresh my memory of that fact every day.

By the time this book is published, I will undoubtedly have reached my fortieth birthday, which is relatively old to be blessed with two young children under the age of six. My wife and I didn't find each other until our late 20s, and we were 30 when we were married.

We also got off to a rather slow beginning in starting a family. Diane had two miscarriages before she finally carried our elder daughter to full term. There was a point in time when we both had to come to grips with the fact that we might never have children. Again, I want to make sure that I remind myself of the incredible blessing of our children.

> **"The soul is healed by being with children."** - Fyodor Dostoevsky

When I think back to the years before we had the girls, I simply can't remember what in the world I thought I was doing that was so important. Today, as I make decisions about every aspect of my life, I first take into consideration the effect it will have on my family. *Is this the best course of action for them?*

In using the words love, nurture, and cherish, I also want to define what they mean to me. Love can mean many different things, but I believe in terms of family, one of the most important aspects of that love is "unconditional acceptance." That's what I choose to practice — being accepting, very appreciative, and as non-judgmental as possible.

Nurturing to me means helping my family members become all they can be. That doesn't include being a dictator (not even a benevolent one). Once my family decides what interests them, and what kinds of dreams they would like to pursue, then it's my job to help them realize those dreams. I want to make sure I give my family all the encouragement, support, and love that is humanly possible.

I must never erect artificial roadblocks, use my family as a kind of whipping post, or take out my frustrations in a thoughtless manner. I choose to make sure I never do or say anything that will damage their self-image and self-esteem.

> **We can apologize for things said in haste and in anger and be very remorseful, but we still can't take those words back.**

I remind myself of that on a regular basis and think before I choose to chastise anyone. One of my strategies is to take a time-out when I become angry. Usually, the less I say, the better off I'll be later.

Lastly, in terms of cherishing my family, I am dedicated to being deeply appreciative of what an incredible gift they are — each of them makes unique contributions to my life. When I use the word cherish, I am reminding myself to not waste any time wishing that a family member would become what I want them to be, or that my goals would become their goals. By doing so, I try to guard against expecting those people to fit into my vision of what might be best for them.

My vision is to appreciate my family for exactly what they are right now, and to remind each one daily of just how important they are in my (and each other's) life.

Now at this point, I fully expect at least half of you to be thinking, "Aw, come on, man, get on with it! All this syrupy sweet, lovey-dovey talk about your family is starting to gag me. Besides, this issue is a no-brainer. Everybody feels that way, don't they?"

In a sense, you are correct on all counts. I am indeed guilty of going after a mosquito with an elephant gun (my way of describing overkill). But possibly the thought with the highest degree of correctness was the no-brainer one. All too often, almost by instinct it would seem, we act as though it were not necessary to engage our brain before dealing with our loved ones.

It is one of the most destructive symptoms of a disease I refer to as "the Human Condition."

It is as if we have a plan to save our worst behavior for those who are the most important to us. To say we take them for granted is to set new standards for understatement.

So, yes, I laid it on a little thick, just as I would apply an antibiotic to a large, open wound. The fact that you and I are what we are (humans), dictates this massive on-going treatment program.

> **" In retrospect, I have no idea what I thought I was doing that was so important . . . before I had kids.**
> - J. Harte

26

PERSPECTIVE # 5

I Recognize My Own Unique Talents

You and I are products of an incredible miracle. here has never been anyone like you or me before, nor will there ever be again. We need to remind ourselves of that fact on a regular basis. We are each a one-of-a-kind combination of genetic traits and environmental influence. There is absolutely no one else like us anywhere in the universe.

> **"Nobody can be exactly like me.**
> **Sometimes even I have trouble doing it."**
> – Tallulah Bankhead

When we are unhappy, or feel sorry for ourselves, we can become completely focused on what we don't have and what we are not. The trouble with this "toxic focus" or "stinking thinking" (as Alcoholics Anonymous calls it), is that we ignore what we do have, and more importantly, what we are. We all need a daily reminder of what a wonderful asset we truly are.

Have you ever thought of yourself as being a championship swimmer? No, you can barely keep yourself from drowning, you say. Well, that may be the case now, but I would like to suggest that at one point in time you were a championship swimmer and, in fact, you won the biggest swimming race of your life, right before conception.

Even if your father had only an average sperm count, you were in a race with at least several tens of millions of sperm, heading for the grand prize, your mother's egg. And you triumphed, you faced your first critical challenge and were up to it. You won the most important race of your existence, or shall we call it pre-existence? You know what I mean.

So now you've won. You got the prize; you got the egg. Now we add another factor into the equation. Human beings have 23 sets of chromosomes, each containing traits from both parents. These sets of chromosomes, equipped with both dominant and recessive traits, comprise our gene pool.

Consider for a moment the mathematical probabilities, before conception, for you to end up being the person that you are today. The fact that you exist, with all your traits, your strengths, your abilities in the order and combination that they occur, is just absolutely astonishing.

People often comment about how children from the same parents can be very different. I know we laugh at our house about the differences in our daughters and wonder out loud, "Can they possibly be from the same gene pool?" And, of course, they are. However, statistics indicate that the probability of two children being very similar is much, much lower than the possibility of them being quite different.

It's good to remind ourselves that we are each uniquely different, realize our strengths, and work to build on them. Don't commiserate with yourself about your perceived liabilities. Get focused on what you are, what you do have, and what assets do exist that come from your genetic background.

You must also understand that your total of acquired abilities, what you have become as a product of your environment, is also a very unique situation. No one has experienced exactly what you have in life. Each hurdle contributes greatly to your present talents and abilities.

We endure and sometimes even triumph over hardships. Every experience has a lasting effect on us.

Every problem, every crisis that comes our way is an opportunity for us to grow. (In fact, these are the times when we do grow and change the most in our lives). Sometimes, at the moment when these events and situations rear their ugly heads, all we can think about is survival. And that may be where our concentrated efforts should be at that specific time. But when the crisis has passed, we are left with a new set of experiences and a greater base of knowledge to draw upon. We will be different and, in fact, we will be better.

In using this perspective I just want to remind myself that there is really nobody like me, and I think, "Hey, that's good." There is no one else with a unique set of chromosomes matched up the way mine are. There is no one who has lived my life. There is no one who has had the exact set of experiences that I've had. (There is no one who has walked a mile in my shoes, if you will.)

If I'm smart, if I'm willing to use former problems in my life as stepping stones to help me handle situations better in the future, then I truly am better prepared to do the right thing, to take the best steps for resolution that are available to me.

When we translate the Chinese character for the word "crisis" into English, it combines two words: "dangerous" and "opportunity." The more literal translation to the Western world would be "a crisis is an opportunity riding a dangerous wind."

Every time we have the opportunity to respond to a crisis or a problem, we can learn and grow from that situation, if we so choose. The sum total of my response to each of the circumstances in my life determines my present level of development.

I don't ever want to wish I were somebody else. I'm grateful that I'm me. I'm grateful for my parents. I'm grateful for my lineage. And, although it's hard to look back at certain events and say, "Boy, I sure am grateful for that rotten thing that happened to me," I do appreciate the experience, and I know I'm better for it.

> **That which does not kill us,
> makes us stronger.**

My Optimism Is My Faith In Action

I enjoy the thoughts of a gentleman named Jim Hansbarger, a successful investment banker, author, and lecturer from Atlanta, Georgia. One concept that he stresses is the development of priority lists.

He believes one area that is often neglected in time management seminars is focusing on the big picture. I agree with him wholeheartedly. It's easy to spend a majority of time focusing on the little things without seeing the big picture. We can become world-class paper-shufflers and paper-clip organizers and still not be headed toward our primary goals.

This story is a favorite of mine. A couple is on vacation. They're speeding down the highway in their rented convertible; the husband is driving while the wife navigates. The husband has a big smile on his face. The wife is turning the map over and over. Finally, exasperated that her husband seems so oblivious to her, she looks over to him and says, "Dear, I'm convinced that we're off course. I can't find the name of that last town anywhere on the map. We're completely lost." The husband glances in her direction, obviously unconcerned; he's simply enjoying the wind in his hair and the sun on his face. "Well, maybe so, honey," he says, "but we're making great time."

That's time management without consideration of your priorities. You may be making great time, but if you don't know where you're going, you might be headed in the wrong direction. That's an incredibly important issue.

Hansbarger also talks about his "Five F's" of priorities. He has tried them in different orders, but the following is best suited for him: Faith. Family. Friends. Fitness (both mental and physical). Finances.

He points out that while individual goals can change from year to year, month to month, or even daily, priorities should essentially remain intact throughout a lifetime. I repeat, goals can change, but priorities should remain pretty darn constant.

> **"The future belongs to those who believe in the beauty of their dreams."**
> - Eleanor Roosevelt

Although it is difficult for me personally to place anything above family, when I stop and give it a little thought, it becomes obvious to me that faith must be the top priority. We all need to have faith in something: faith in God, faith in ourselves, faith in the system, faith in our family structure, faith that we are going through life doing the right things. Faith is mandatory for a healthy and productive life. The absence of faith is despair.

Imagine for a moment that you are an enthusiastic football fan. (This will be easier for some of you than for others, but please give it a try.) Picture yourself watching your favorite team getting creamed during the first half of the big game. Feel the pain, the frustration, the anxiety of seeing the blunders. The missed opportunities and the backfired strategies steal the joy from what had promised to be a day filled with glory. Sucks the life right out of you, doesn't it?

But wait, stop right there. The game isn't over. Your team makes a great comeback in the second half and wins a close, hard-played game. Oh, the relief, the exhilaration, the satisfaction — the exhaustion.

You would have been much better off if you had watched a taped replay of the game, knowing the outcome ahead of time. That first half would still have been somewhat painful to live through, but the toll it would have exacted on you (both physically and mentally) would have been much smaller.

Having faith as we go through life is much like watching that football game on tape. There are going to be a number of problems and difficult situations that will test us at times. But if I know that in the end things are going to turn out like they're supposed to, I can cope. I can address those problems as they come along much more calmly, peacefully, and with much less pain. In fact, when I'm in that more relaxed, calm, and peaceful state, I'm actually going to handle those situations better.

> **With faith,
> anything is possible.**

Optimism to me is the action step of having faith. The converse of optimism, of course, is pessimism, and I think pessimism gets way too much publicity.

Chuck Daly was a very successful professional basketball coach in Detroit a few years ago. He was referred to in the newspapers as "The Prince of Pessimism." He was always anticipating the worst.

Daly himself would give this quote to newspaper reporters on a regular basis, "That's right; I'm a pessimist. That's an optimist with experience."

Well, I don't buy it. I don't believe that Mr. Daly was a pessimist at all. He worked tirelessly to be prepared for any situation. His title of "Prince of Pessimism" was false. If he were truly a pessimist, Mr. Daly would never call a timeout to talk to his team about the game. He would never make a substitution. "Why bother? The next guy won't do any better anyway." In fact, Mr. Daly would never even show up for another game. "What's the use? We're going to lose."

He wasn't a pessimist at all. He was indeed "The Prince of Preparedness."

When faith is high on our priority list, we give optimism a fighting chance to bring about the actions that bear out that faith. Optimism is indeed our faith in action. Being optimistic makes a statement about our faith to the world and to ourselves – hopefully, we will be listening.

I Am Solution-Oriented

This Perspective is simply an extension of the previous one. It deals mainly with optimism. If we are optimistic about the eventual outcome of events, we will actively look for solutions to difficult situations. I believe that people in general can be divided into two groups: many are problem-oriented, while the rest are solution-oriented. I believe whether you are pessimistic or optimistic is the primary basis for that orientation.

Pessimistic people don't really need to look for solutions because even if they find one, they won't believe it will work. (Ironically, these folks will often work their tails off to prove that something won't work.) Optimistic people, on the other hand, know that finding solutions will help them rectify and improve situations in their life.

I also believe there is a biological reason why we benefit from being solution-oriented: a part of our brain called the Reticular Activating System (R.A.S.). Biologists tell us that this portion of the brain, located at the back of the head and near the base of the neck, performs a rather low brain function. I personally think that although it may be a lower function, it is also one of the most important.

The R.A.S. focuses the filter that our brain uses to tune out a majority of the barrage of sensory inputs that we constantly receive. We have five senses of which we are acutely aware, and all five of them are receiving input around the clock. If the R.A.S. didn't filter out some of it, we would be so confused that we would never accomplish anything.

Hopefully, you're concentrating on reading the words in this book, so you're most sensitized to your sense of sight. If I ask you to become aware of the clothing that is touching your arms, you can do that. If I ask you to become aware of the seat that you're sitting on pressing up against the back of your legs at this moment, you can also become aware of that.

Yet, in the moments just previous to my suggesting you become aware of those things, you probably were oblivious to them — it was almost as if you were naked, suspended in midair. It's important to be able to filter out some sensations so we can really concentrate on one thing at a time.

The R.A.S. works on a priority basis. We determine areas that are important and it directs the filter.

Think of it as working like the fine tuner on your car radio. If you hop in your car, turn on the radio, and only get a blast of static, the tuner is probably on a setting where no station is broadcasting. Immediately you start tuning in various stations: a country singer lamenting the fact that his girlfriend has left him high and dry; the weather report (and if you're from Michigan like I am, you know it's good only for about 10 minutes); elevator music that could lull you back to sleep; a screaming rock 'n' roll star. So far, nothing you want to listen to. Finally, you settle on a station that's tolerable.

The next question is, "Are those other stations that you chose not to listen to still broadcasting?" Of course they are. Can you hear them? Can you hear more than one of them at one time? No, you can't. The fine tuner zeros your radio in on just one signal. In essence, that's how your R.A.S. works. And, a big part of how your R.A.S. gets tuned in to your different senses has much to do with your orientation towards solutions or problems.

Here's a little secret of life I'd like to share: You find what you look for. People who look for problems have no trouble finding them. Bad news sells. People like to spread the dirt, and we want to know it. Just pick up any newspaper. The reason bad news is placed on the front page is because it sells newspapers.

Bad news not only sells, but it also is the path of least resistance. It's easy to get down and wallow in self-pity with other people and moan, "What a horrible world we live in." Finding problems is no problem.

Solutions, on the other hand, take a little work, a little more creativity, more of a commitment to success. The good news is that if solutions are what you're looking for, that's what you'll find. Problems and solutions are out there waiting to be tuned in, just like the radio waves from all the different stations broadcasting. Remember, you control the tuner.

I remind myself of that fact and renew the commitment to be optimistic and solution-oriented every day. When I am in that mode on a regular basis, solutions are exactly what I find.

> **"The answer my friend,**
> **is blowin' in the wind."**
> - Bob Dylan

PERSPECTIVE # 8

I Use My Power of Choice Wisely

I believe one of the mistakes we make in life is forgetting exactly how much control we really do exert over outcomes. We do have the power of choice, but too often we fail to exercise it. I enjoy revisiting the full scope of choices that I have in life on a daily basis.

If I were to write my own epitaph, it would include the following phrase stating what I would hope to be remembered as always being aware of: "The 'stuff' in our lives is not nearly as important as how we respond to it."

We always have the power to choose our response. Very often, we abdicate that power by not making a choice. In reality, failing to make a decision is a decision in itself — deciding not to do anything. In my opinion, inaction is often the cowardly approach.

A powerful message I recall receiving came from one of the first self-help books I ever read, *Your Erroneous Zones*, by Dr. Wayne Dyer. He writes: "At this point in time you are nothing more or less than the sum total of all the choices you have made in your life."

If you don't like where you are in your life, if you don't like your occupation, your level of education, or your family structure, what you need to remember is that you are a result of the choices you've made. That's the bad news.

But here's the good news: Five years from now you will also be the sum total of the choices you've made. So you've got five years to start making good choices. As a matter of fact, you can start making a difference in your life today by simply becoming aware of all the choices that really are available to you.

In the past, I had the unproductive habit of trying to abdicate responsibility for some of my actions, particularly in relationships, by saying, "I can't help it; it's how I feel. I can't control my feelings; it's my gut feeling." I would use this as an excuse in making poor choices about handling situations with significant others.

Dr. Dyer points out the error in this kind of thinking when he says, "We control our thoughts. Our feelings come from our thoughts. Therefore, we control our feelings." It took me a long time to buy into this, but now that I have, I know that I am much more in control of my feelings than I was before.

Our feelings are basically the internalized responses linked to our thoughts which are in response to stimulus from the world. No one can hurt our feelings without our permission and cooperation. In other words, we are choosing to think in ways that are painful and hurtful to us when we respond in this way to people who say things that "hurt our feelings."

(This is a component of today's immensely popular "Blame Game." Teflon-coated suits of armor have become the apparel of choice for a segment of our society, which seems to be growing at an exponential rate. Note: Watch 10 minutes of any of the umpteen talk shows— if you have the stomach for it — for confirmation of this alarming situation. These apparently attention-starved individuals are a study in the result of victim mentality. But, I digress — this is a battle to be fought on other pages.)

The power of choice is one of our greatest gifts. I try to include a thought of gratitude about this gift when I say daily prayers. First I give thanks to God for this life, this incredible roller-coaster ride; second, for the people in my life who are such a great influence on me; and for my wonderful gift of family. Then I like to remind myself that these gifts come from God — no strings attached. We have been given the power of choice. We choose the way that we respond to these gifts and to being on this Earth. That's a very powerful position.

Of course, with power comes responsibility. We have the power of choice. But we need to make sure that we don't abuse it; that we don't lose it through inaction; and that we use it wisely.

> **"Even if you're on the right track, you'll get run over if you sit there."**
> – Will Rogers

I Assure My Success by Always Going the Extra Mile

This is one of my favorite Perspectives. I remind myself that in doing the little things in life, I make the big difference. I believe it's not that tough to stand out today because we have so many people in our world who are looking for shortcuts, the easy way out. They want success to be quick, painless, and easy.

Many people display the attitude that, "I deserve success because I was born in the United States. My parents have told me I was special since the minute I could understand the language. I want the American dream and I want it now." (I refer to this as the Entitlement Myth.) Far too many people are interested only in minimum standards and minimum effort — yet expect the maximum rewards.

I believe you can also recognize this philosophy in the management style used by a large number of people. It's been encouraged by what I call a "union mentality." It is based on a relationship between unions and management that revolves around minimum standards. When *minimums* are the main focus, they soon become *maximums* for performance. Doing the minimum is just not good enough to be successful in today's global marketplace.

The opposite theory involves staying focused on doing the little extra things. We can differentiate ourselves from the rest of the pack by being the person (or organization) that always makes the extra effort; the one that puts the personal touch on things whenever possible. I send out thank-you notes that include little books. It costs a little extra, but I know that people remember me when they make decisions about hiring lecturers and staff trainers.

I often telephone people to set up appointments for phone calls (that really wows people) because I want to ensure that the important conversation we are about to have is at a time that is convenient for both of us. I don't assume that because someone answers the telephone they have time for me right at that minute. To me, that's another way of going the extra mile.

Our attention to detail is a signal to others that we are very thorough, that we are going to do a heck of a good job, that our follow-up is excellent and timely, and that excellence is high on our priority list.

One nice thing about going the extra mile is that it's not very crowded. It's relatively easy to separate yourself because most people are much more focused on the minimum requirements than they are on performing to the best of their abilities.

One arena where this is very evident is in the world of athletics. The people who are doing the extra repetitions, the extra training, the extra weight work, the extra conditioning are definitely the people who are successful. These are people who create their own luck.

Go the extra mile; cover every base; make sure every detail is addressed — if you sweat the small stuff, the big stuff will take care of itself.

Assure your success by always going the extra mile.

**There is little traffic
on the extra mile.**

PERSPECTIVE # 10

I Spend Most of My Time On Things That Are Important, But Not Urgent

This Perspective again comes directly from the brilliant work of Dr. Steven Covey, who, I believe will be recognized as one of the greatest self-help, personal-management gurus of all time. In his book, *The Seven Habits of Highly Effective People*, Dr. Covey lists this as one of his secondary habits: Spend most of your time on things that are important, but not urgent.

Pictured below is my interpretation of Dr. Covey's time-management matrix. We can place everything we do into it, based on two factors: urgency and importance.

Quadrant #1	Quadrant #2
IMPORTANT AND URGENT medical emergencies perceived crises large brush fires an angry boss dissatisfied customers important things ignored	IMPORTANT, BUT NOT URGENT strategic planning, organization nurturing children education, training exercise, rest and relaxation personal, emotional & spiritual development preventive maintenance regular dental checkups
Quadrant #3	Quadrant #4
NOT IMPORTANT, BUT URGENT ringing phone other people's agendas small brush fires	NOT IMPORTANT AND NOT URGENT gossip most television tabloids, rumor mill magazines borrowing trouble second guessing

As you can see, items listed under "Important, But Not Urgent" are some of the real keys to success in life. Things (from Quadrant #2) that are ignored eventually end up in Quadrant #1. That's when they become important <u>and</u> urgent.

If these are truly important aspects of our life, we should deal with them long before they become urgent. When things become urgent they tend to set off the stress response. We may rush into things without proper preparation. We simply will not be at our best and will often produce results that indicate, "It is the best I can do in the time that was given." Often, through procrastination, we create circumstances for ourselves where we don't do a job that we are proud of simply because we did not give ourselves enough time to do the job properly.

When we work on items before they become urgent, we are much more relaxed. We have time to deal with the inevitable questions that arise for which we don't have answers. We can do a thorough job. We can edit. We can rewrite. We can get more information. We can seek advice. We can make a trial run and then adjust and be much happier with the final product. If the items are truly important, shouldn't we work for the best possible result? I think so.

> **"We can do anything we want if we stick to it long enough."**
> – Helen Keller

I also make sure that working on things on this list (Quadrant #2) is a big part of how I spend my time. I don't want to reserve this for a special few minutes a day and spend the rest of my time on busy work. If that happens, I will be putting out brush fires all day.

Putting out fires, doing busy work, keeping occupied without really working on the items that are part of my long-range goals will not help me be successful in the long run. I remind myself that the majority of my time should be spent on items that are important and that I need to address these items before they become urgent, while I'm calm, relaxed, pleasant, and able to do my best.

PERSPECTIVE # 11

I Seek First To Understand

This may be thought of as the "communication" Perspective. It is designed to remind me that listening must be number one on my list of necessary skills in order to develop good communication with others.

All people have a very strong, almost instinctive need to feel that they are being heard and that their concerns are understood by others. By being a great listener, we can address and meet that need. It's also probable that when we attempt to really understand another person's point of view, we are more likely to be successful at presenting our own ideas in a way that is relevant to the person with whom we're communicating.

Relevance is a very important factor in terms of listening. If the first words we hear indicate the topic doesn't hold much importance for us, our listening skills immediately diminish. It is vitally important that I make my information relevant to your life.

In a program of mine called "The Lost Art of Listening," I stress the fact that in order to be a good listener, we must have a firm grasp on being open to other points of view. Without that feeling of openness, nearly anything someone says has the potential to turn off our listening skills. We may begin to listen to our inner voice and make value judgments that may keep us from being a good listener and distract us from retaining much of the information.

We should also keep in mind that other people do the same

thing to us. When we are judgmental, when we want to give advice using a snap judgment, we turn other peoples' listening systems off.

Once again, the most important part of listening and communicating is making sure that we comprehend everything we can about the other person's point of view, before we attempt to have that person see things from our perspective.

> **"LLLUUUCCCYYY!!!**
> **You got some 'splaining to do."**
> – Ricky Ricardo

Another Perspective that is not included in this list, but which does fit in nicely with this one, is "I learn something from everyone I meet." When I realize that my goal is to learn something from each person I I come in contact with, I'm less likely to be judgmental and turn off my inner listening skills. I'm much more likely to make associations with the items the person is talking about so that I can ask informed questions.

A good phrase to integrate into your everyday conversation is one that seeks to clarify what other people have just stated. Something like, "Now let's see, if I understand you correctly..." and then repeat what you think you heard. When we do this, when we repeat what other people say in different words and ask them to put it in other ways, hopefully we will get a very clear picture of exactly what that person was trying to communicate.

I have also discovered that this strategy improves my ability to listen dramatically. Knowing in advance that I will be repeating what I just heard helps me get control of my internal "self-chatter" and enhances my ability to get a "laser-focus" on the other person's words and ideas.

When we repeat back what has been said, we demonstrate that we have been listening carefully, and we give value to the expressed ideas. In a small way, that raises self-esteem and increases cooperation. This is a form of team-building that is a very good approach to communicating with people.

All this information can be distilled into one little phrase: I seek first to understand. When I do this, when I communicate with an understanding of the other person's ideas, I automatically upgrade the quality of our communication and diminish the chance of incorrectly interpreting what someone else is saying.

I Say "No" When It Is Necessary

As much as we'd like to be, sometimes we simply cannot be all things to all people. Sometimes we have to say no. Sometimes, we may say no by saying, "Yes, I'm already engaged at that time," or "Yes, I already have a commitment that I must keep."

Earl Nightingale tells a story in one of his cassette magazine series entitled "Insight" that suggests a way to tell people that we are already occupied or committed, or that we simply don't have the time to fulfill their request in a quality manner. He says that their request has crossed the Pensal line.

According to Nightingale's story, in the 1600s and 1700s, greedy European merchants, who were trying to make the biggest profit possible, would load their ships beyond a safe capacity. If the crew and the ship were lucky enough to experience fair weather on the voyage, they made it safely. If they encountered a storm or rough weather, the ship often went down because it was overloaded. Much cargo and the lives of many men were lost in this manner.

Because of the immense profit that could be gained, the merchants were willing to take a chance with their merchandise and the lives of the crew. It was certainly not a fair situation for the crew members, many of whom were in such dire economic straights that they were forced to work, even if it meant there was a chance they could die.

A member of the English Parliament at the time, named Pensal, initiated legislation that stated each boat had to be studied by engineers and a limit established for how much weight the ship could safely carry. Once this weight limit was established, the boat was loaded to the set weight and a line was painted marking the point where the water came on the boat — the Pensal line.

When a merchant ship was being loaded, all the crew and cargo was loaded until the Pensal line touched the water. Once that happened, not one more bit of cargo was allowed to be loaded and the ship left port with an appropriate load.

Nightingale's point is, once you are loaded to your safe maximum, any new request for your time, energies, or your abilities to work on a project must be considered as crossing that Pensal line. It's a unique way to tell people, "Hey, I believe that your project bears merit, but I am just unable to do it justice at this time. It hurts me to turn you down, but I must."

> **"Time is the coin of your life.**
> **Be careful lest you let other**
> **people spend it for you."**
> – Carl Sandburg

As I said before, sometimes we simply cannot be all things to all people. I believe it's much better to focus on a smaller number of projects and do a thorough, complete job on each one that we do undertake.

In order to do this, we need to understand what some of our limits are. We need to have signals — I call them red flags — that we are overburdening ourselves by taking on too many projects. For me, that often is a harried sort of a feeling. My anxiety level will rise slowly but surely, and very often when I'm trying to accomplish too much, my red flag will be a change (for the worse) in my vocabulary.

Under normal circumstances I have high regard for the English language and the ears upon which it falls. However, there are times when I am anxious or feel pressured by the number of projects I have undertaken, that a few unsavory words creep into my vocabulary. Hopefully, this only happens somewhere other than in the presence of my daughters — I'm not trying to expand their vocabulary in that direction.

When I hear something foul come out of my mouth, it's a signal, "Hey, you've got too much going on the front burner. Some things are going to have to be moved to the back of the stove. Get yourself more in line with the amount of work that you can handle and still do a good job on each item."

It's also a time when I really need to exercise the suggestion in this Perspective. I absolutely need to say no, unless something is vitally important. If I must say yes, I've got to make certain that I rearrange my schedule to make sure that the projects on my upcoming agenda are things I really need to do.

We all need to learn to say no — when necessary.

> **"A heart attack doesn't care if you won at Wimbledon or lost in your own back yard."**
> – Arthur Ashe

PERSPECTIVE # 13

I Change My Approach When
Seeking Different Results

With this Perspective, I remind myself that doing more of the same will just get me more of the same results. Put another way: If you keep on doing what you've always done, you'll keep on getting what you've always gotten.

Too often we become mired in a mental mode where we tell ourselves that we are doing things the right way; it's circumstances beyond our control that are adversely affecting results.

Some famous last words: "This is the way that I have always done it; it's the way my dad did it before me and his dad before him." "It's the way my previous boss did things; it's the way the previous owners did things and it brought them good results in the past; so we just need to do more; we need to work harder; and longer." Very often, I'm afraid, this just is not correct. We don't need to work harder; we need to work smarter.

> ### GOOD WORKING DEFINITION #4
> *Insanity* —Doing things the same way
> you always have, and expecting the
> results to be different.

I like a little phrase that encourages me to get going, not wait for perfection or the perfect idea before I get started on a project.

The Nike people in their advertisements encourage us to "just do it." Just get started.

Tom Peters, business management guru and author of *In Search of Excellence* and many other bestselling books about business management says, "One of the mistakes we make is that we think that if we simply think long enough and hard enough and plan properly, that in fact we can predict in advance where lightning will strike."

If we stop and think in terms like that, we know it's crazy. We simply cannot do that. Yet that is often how we act. Peters implies that we just need to get going, just get started.

I've also heard another interesting phrase used in a couple of different ways. I've heard people make reference to the Japanese as they try to analyze some of our management styles, and I've heard one author say that the Japanese make fun of Americans because we do things in this order: ready, fire, aim. That's not the way it should be. We should get ready; we should aim very carefully, and then fire.

A different author has said the Japanese admire this; they think ready, fire, aim, is, in fact, a good approach. I happen to agree with them. We just need to get started. It's not required that we are able to predict in advance exactly where lightning is going to strike. Let's just get started and see how things shake out; let's see where the interest is; let's see what's successful.

A good approach for beginning basic strategic planning for your life or in a project is to figure out which ideas are currently working and which ones are not. Then take that information and simply plan to do more of what is working and less of what is not. Very often, we fail to view strategies in such a simplistic manner. We are stuck in our present paradigms and continue doing things the same way they have always been done without ever knowing why.

If I view my approach to things as my mental road map and the desired results as the destination, it becomes easier for me to concede that if I seek a new destination (different results), I must be willing to use a different map (change the approach).

I Feel Great About Choosing Foods
That Are Good For Me

   This Perspective is somewhat different from some of
the rest in that it is designed specifically to change the way I have
thought about healthy foods in the past and help me realize a better
mind-set about choosing more nutritious foods. It's like opting to use a
new and improved mental road map.

   In the past I have been a world-class dieter. During my lifetime,
I have lost hundreds of pounds. My problem has been that I have
gained back all those hundreds, plus fifty. This roller-coaster ride that
my weight has been on for almost 35 years has been one of the greatest
distractions in my life.

   Looking back at my dietary patterns, I realized that during the
times when I was losing weight, I put my nose to the grindstone, so to
speak, and through sheer willpower ate foods that I didn't like, ate very
small amounts, and spent a lot of time feeling hungry and deprived.
Often when I was in a dieting period, I was making healthy choices for
food, but in essence I was still feeling like I was really suffering, being
deprived of the food that I actually wanted.

   I spent too much time thinking, "When I get off this diet, I'm
going to go back to eating chocolate and chili dogs and potato chips."
These foods were really not very healthy for me, but they made me feel
good, not from a physical standpoint, but from a mental standpoint. My
wife very appropriately calls some of these items "comfort foods."

One of the necessary mind-set changes I had to make was to feel differently about healthy food. I needed to become less resentful about buying foods that were good for me. It is very important that I only buy healthy foods and simply not have comfort foods available around the house, (in the event I should suffer from a moment of weakness.) That's a tough buying pattern to change.

> **"Adam and Eve ate the first vitamins;**
> **including the package."**
> – E. R. Squibb

In the grocery store, I try to be very conscious of the healthy choices I make. I have a list prepared that includes only healthy foods. While I'm purchasing those foods and putting items in my basket, I make sure that I remind myself that these are choices that will benefit my health and energy levels in the future.

When I pick up that healthy food, that head of lettuce, those golden delicious applies, the bananas, the whole-grain, low-fat, and no-fat products — I use this Perspective to reinforce just how good it feels. I'm in control here; I'm making choices that are good for me now and in the future; and I take a moment to give myself a little pat on the back.

I really do feel awfully good about this Perspective. It reinforces a feeling of increased self-control and increased self-discipline that also lets me feel comfortable and confident about the future.

For me, this is a most important Perspective. It really has worked quite well for me in changing my attitude about healthy foods.

> **"Cut out those little intimate dinners for**
> **two, unless there's someone with you."**
> – Joey Adams

Water Is My Fitness Drink,
and I Drink Lots Of It

On the whole, we just don't drink enough water in this country. That's rather ironic because we have one of the best water supplies anywhere in the world.

First of all, how much is enough water? Let's start with 64 ounces. That's a half-gallon of water a day, which is considered a minimum requirement for every adult. Add to that eight more ounces of water for every 20 minutes of vigorous workout. Now, consumption at those levels is having water as your fitness drink.

Water is such an important part of the body. Depending on which model you choose, the human body is anywhere from 80 to 95 percent water. I like the analogy that water is to our muscles as oil is to the motor in your automobile — it's what allows it to operate properly, keeps it loose, cool, and deters it from breaking down.

> **Water is to your muscles
> as oil is to your car's engine.**

Water is also a factor in mental toughness because when we become dehydrated, the stress response is triggered much more easily. This is a key component to success and happiness, so let's drink enough water for the mental health of it.

If water is so important, why we don't drink enough water in our society? Reason number one: Water is just not very spectacular. It's odorless, colorless, and tasteless. It's simply not very exciting. There's no fizz, no bubbles. Let's face it. Water is boring. (Heaven knows there's no room in the fast lane for anything that can be described by the B-word.)

A second reason could be that it's just not convenient to drink the proper amount of water. Let me ask you a rhetorical question. (Rhetorical means, I'm not looking for an answer.) That question is: If tomorrow you decided to adopt this policy and start drinking at least a half-gallon of water a day, which would be far beyond your normal practice, where would you spend most of the day? In the bathroom, right? Hey, you don't have time for that sort of thing. So now water is not only boring, but it's inconvenient.

Here's another rhetorical question: If you did in fact spend a significantly larger portion of time in the bathroom facilities, what would you be doing there? YOU WOULD BE FLUSHING TOXINS FROM YOUR BODY. That's how the system is designed to work. That's how we rid our body of the poisons and by-products that we produce and the toxins we take in along with the good nutrition — by flushing these things through our kidneys.

There are two chances that you are drinking enough water, slim and none. Without a specific water consumption strategy, most of us fall victim to a self-induced state of mild dehydration. We can literally become a walking cesspool.

Keep that model in your mind – a walking cesspool. If you want to get yourself flushed out, if you want to be physically clean and mentally healthy, drink enough water, please. Start with 64 ounces a day, add to that total as you exercise, and you'll be doing yourself a great service.

There's also one other matter you might want to take into consideration. Since the 1920s, there have been nearly 30,000 diet plans documented. I have not reviewed all 30,000 of them, (although it seems like I've tried most of them), but I would be very willing to bet my next year's income that the most common element in those diet plans is the consumption of large quantities of water.

So there's a lot of good news about water: It's one of our best natural resources; it's cheap; the increased level of fitness awareness has made good drinking water available at every grocery and convenience store in America. Hey! You want to be more physically fit without a lot of effort? Start drinking more water. You want to be more mentally tough tomorrow than you were today? Drink more water.

I know this sounds complicated (just kidding). C'mon, what are you waiting for? With all due apologies to Nike — Just drink it!

> **"Without a specific water drinking strategy, we will most likely create a state of self-induced dehydration — and essentially become a walking cesspool."** - J. Harte

My Workouts Are the
Best Part of My Day

When I consider the various fitness programs that I've been involved in over the years, the successes I experienced were never permanent. I enjoyed some success, but only on a temporary basis.

In looking at those programs, I considered two matters: one was my nutrition plan, or "dieting," and the other was my exercise plan. I discovered that I had been attempting to make those programs work by what I would refer to as willpower. "I know it's the right thing to do; I'll enjoy the results, but I really don't want to do them."

I now understand that the results from the change in my habit behavior will be short-lived as long as I continue to resent and not enjoy my workout periods. I need to strengthen my resolve that my workouts are the best part of my day.

Today, once I get into my workouts, I really do believe this. It becomes an excellent part of my day, maybe even the best part. But, it always helps to remind myself of the wonderful things I'm doing for myself and of the good things that happen to me as a result of workouts: my old habit of skipping workouts is quickly replaced by an overwhelming desire to get started.

Without daily workouts, my back tightens up. I have trouble driving any great distance because of the tightness in my back, and travel is a big part of my work. My workouts also raise my metabolism. That means I get the furnace to burn a little hotter. I will burn the food that I consume more efficiently, and in turn, my body is going to have less fat-storage from the foods that I eat.

> **"If I had known I was going to live this long, I would have taken better care of myself."** - Mickey Mantle
> (and most of the rest of us)

Workouts really clear my head. My thought processes become much clearer and in sync. I've been mentally compiling articles for this book during my workout periods (which include walking, swimming, biking, etc.).

When I take into consideration all the benefits that result from my daily workouts, it becomes clear that this time is one of the most productive and effective parts of my day. It improves my performance, outlook, attitude, patience, and lowers my stress levels. My workouts really are the best part of my day. Reminding myself of that helps keep workouts high on my daily priority list.

In essence, workouts are working on yourself from a physical standpoint to improve your PC, your production capability. Insisting that you take time for your workouts — which can mean making time in your schedule that takes you away from your family, job, etc. — may sometimes seem selfish. You need to remember this: If you do not take the time to take care of yourself and to make sure that your production capability is at its highest level, you're going to have less and less to offer other people who really need your significant contributions.

Dr. Steven Covey refers to this issue of self-renewal as "sharpening the saw." We must keep the saw (or axe) sharp if we're going to cut down the trees, if we're going to make contributions in a positive, efficient manner.

I have developed a mind-set that works well for me and fits nicely with this information. In the past, when I had a very busy schedule or a number of deadlines looming, I would justify skipping my workout, saying, "Hey, I've got too much to do today. Missing one day won't bother me." That was my old paradigm, my old pattern of thinking.

My new paradigm says, "I have too much to do today to be able to afford to skip my workout. It is paramount that I get my workout in today because I have to be at my best." This paradigm shift has helped me immensely.

When I take the time to view the big picture, to consider the positive impact this use of my time has on my health, well-being, and productivity, it becomes easy to see that "My workouts are the best part of my day" (and can quickly become the best part of your day, too).

My Body is Lean and Flexible

This Perspective attempts to underscore a slightly different outlook on two matters that to me have been somewhat overlooked in the realm of physical fitness. The first, "My body is lean," refers to the percentages of weight that are body fat and lean muscle mass.

We've all seen charts in doctor's waiting rooms that show if you're 5 foot 8 inches and have a small, medium, or heavy frame, your weight should be within a certain range. That doesn't take into account muscle mass at all; it's just an average assessment. (Note: I personally no longer look at those charts and think of myself as being overweight; I'm just seven inches too short).

While these charts may be better than no reference at all, they fail to take into account what the medical and health community can now effectively measure; the percentage of weight that is fat. In general, the standards for body fat percentages for good levels of fitness are 12 percent for men and 18 percent for women. These are nice targets. If you feel you're even slightly overweight, your body fat percentage is probably going to be somewhat higher than those figures.

A discouraging aspect of a reducing diet is this: People feel that they're making progress — their pants are looser around their waist; they feel more fit and have more energy, but they don't see the results on the scales when they weigh themselves. What they have to remember is that muscle mass weighs more than fat. If we have an intelligent exercise program as part of our weight-reduction regime, we're going to build more muscles and so may not see the immediate weight loss we had hoped for. Sometimes we may even see an increase in weight.

What we have to keep in mind is that we are reducing our body fat, and that is an important standard of success, one that should always be one of our goals. Rather than saying, "I want to get my weight down to 165 pounds," you might say, "I want to get my body fat down to 10 percent."

The other half of the Perspective refers to flexibility. Flexibility (or range of motion) is an area that makes a very strong statement about our overall level of fitness. One consideration that should be high on anyone's overall fitness program should be to reduce the chance of injury. Very often injuries, particularly for the non-athlete, come from putting our body in an awkward position or in any position that strains muscles that have been disused.

I once heard the concept of flexibility described as, "The less flexible we become, the smaller our range of motion, the closer we are to *rigor mortis*." That really hit home from me. The saying, "If you don't use it, you lose it," really applies to your flexibility and range of motion.

The other positive aspect about flexibility is that in order to maintain and/or increase your flexibility and range of motion, you will need to participate in activities that will also help you reduce stress (stretching, yoga, etc.) Whoa! Now we're approaching holistic fitness. (And you thought that would be painful!)

This Perspective forces me to think about how much fat I carry around (which has a lot to do with how much energy I have); how I handle the foods that I intake, and what kind of a load I am placing on my heart. The flexibility part refers to trying to resist *rigor mortis*. This simple reminder is going to trigger my thoughts in a couple of important (but often overlooked) fitness-related areas.

> **"You know you're getting old when you stoop to tie your shoes and wonder what else you can do while you're down there."** - George Burns

My Resting Pulse Is Under Sixty

Monitoring and measuring the progress of your resting pulse is a marvelous way to gain insight into the fitness level of the most important muscle in your body — your heart. The number of times your heart beats each minute as blood moves through your circulatory system is a wonderful indicator of the overall health of your cardiovascular system. I have chosen 60 as my target number.

One of the most commonly asked questions on this issue is: "What is the average resting pulse?" Most doctors say that an average resting pulse is in the mid to low 70s.

Now, if a doctor were to tell me that the condition of my heart was average, I would begin to panic. Why? Because heart-related diseases are the number one cause of death in this country. When a doctor says, "You're average," in essence he's telling you, "Hey, you're headed for a nice, normal death due to heart failure or stroke or some other circulatory-related problem."

I don't want my heart to be average in health — I want my heart to be well *above* average.

I enjoy listening to a speaker named "Zig" Ziglar, who boasts of having had a resting pulse of 40 when he was in his early 60s. That's way down on the other end of the spectrum. Forty is obviously an excellent heart rate, usually only seen in marathoners and professional bicycle racers. I would like to be under 60, in the high to mid-50s. That number indicates a pretty good level of fitness. It might be a level of fitness that a professional baseball player would want to attain.

Athletes involved in endurance-type sports, such as basketball or hockey, are more likely to be in the low 50s or high 40s. Long distance runners, triathletes, and bicycle racers are going to be in the low 40s.

I have always been interested in the measurements of fitness that are done on bicyclists who ride in the *Tour de France*, the most famous bicycle race in the world. The race requires four to eight hours of racing, 23 out of 24 consecutive days. Usually, the heart rate of the winner is in the very high 30s, and the announcer will make some sort of comment like, "We had to wake this guy up to tell him that he won the low resting heart rate contest."

I don't think you need to attain a pulse rate in the 30s or 40s to exhibit good fitness. I believe that a rate in the 60s is not only a good target, but is attainable. You won't have to become a marathon runner to achieve a resting pulse near 60.

Suppose you take your resting pulse a few mornings in a row and observe, "Wow, it's almost 80. I'm in really terrible shape. I have a long way to go." A reassuring fact about resting heart rate is that the higher it is, the easier it is to get it down. In other words, going from 80 to 70 will be a much easier issue than going from 70 to 65.

Using myself as an example, as I often measure in the low 60s, I have to do a fair amount of work just to maintain that resting heart rate of near 60. To get it from 60 to 58 or 57 is going to take substantially greater efforts.

An interesting side benefit of a reduced resting heart rate is the savings of total heart beats accumulated in a year's time. Suppose you reduce your resting heart rate 10 beats per minute, down to 60. If you calculate the number of heart beats of a person with a pulse of 60, the total for an entire year would be roughly 32.5 million heart beats.

If your present resting pulse is in the mid-70 range, and you reduce it 10 beats per minute, you will save over 5.5 million beats per year. That's a big number — pretty good results!

Now, stop and consider an individual whose heart rate is in the low 80s, instead of our original number of the low 70s, and develop the concept in the opposite direction. Imagine it as giving away 10 heart-beats a minute. That person's heart is going to beat an extra 5.5 million times per year — that's a significant issue.

No one has ever seen a warranty on the heart muscle, but we know the scope of its use is not endless.

So for me, personally, I try to keep my resting pulse in the 60 range, even under 60 if possible. If I do that, after 20 years I will have saved 110 million heartbeats, which will add three years to my heart's warranty.

That may be a quirky way to view the issue, but I know that resting pulse is one of the easiest and most important fitness evaluation functions that you can do for yourself. Start tracking it. The best time is first thing in the morning, before you get out of bed.

Take this one seriously, please.

When your doctor tells you your heart is average, feel free to panic. It means you are on the path to a nice, normal death by heart disease.

PERSPECTIVE # 19

I Stretch My Body Every Day

If outstanding flexibility is one of my goals
(and it is), stretching every day is the way to achieve
that end result.

Stretching, increasing your range of motion, should be done on
a very consistent basis. It is also an area that should involve slow,
gradual progress. Trying to achieve quick progress in range-of-motion
can result in an injury, a muscle tear or a tendon strain. It must be done
gradually and consistently.

Along with increased range-of-motion, stress reduction is a
natural by-product of stretching. Static tension builds in muscles when
we are physically inactive. Anxiety and frustration can amplify existing
muscle tension. The body senses this, and stress response intensifies. In
the worst case scenario, we can create an escalating spiral of stress-
response fallout (first physical, then mental, then physical...) that may
become almost self-perpetuating. Stretching our muscles releases static
tension and breaks the cycle. Regular practitioners often come to the
comforting realization that they are capable of not only breaking the
cycle, but that they can actually reverse it.

My belief is that the slow, deliberate, relatively passive nature
of a good stretching program, combined with the quickly achieved
physical pleasure and feelings of accomplishment, can lead directly
to a calming, peaceful effect on the mind. But, hey, that's just my
experience. Try it for yourself.

Keep in mind that the results you achieve from stretching can be lost in a fairly short period of time if the activity isn't continued on a regular basis. It's a good idea to develop a program that fits into a daily time slot.

I would also recommend using a stretching video tape or a beginning Yoga video. This type of video will outline various exercises for you to follow and help you develop a routine. Then adhere to that schedule of stretching on a regular basis. Warning: Feelings of well-being can become addictive.

> **The more range of motion we lose,
> the closer we get to rigor mortis.**

I Stretch My Mind Every Day

The mind, once stretched by a new idea, will never return to its original shape. I really love that thought. The concept that we have the capability for constant learning and intellectual growth is really exciting to me.

There's a story that's often told about a gentleman who saw U.S. Supreme Court Justice Oliver Wendell Holmes, then in his 90s, reading in the court's library. "What are you doing, sir?" the man asked. The judge replied "I'm reading Plato." The fellow asked, "Why are you reading Plato?" Justice Holmes looked at him incredulously and said, "To improve my mind."

We're never too old to learn; it's never too late to begin exploring new intellectual frontiers.

I have fond memories of my grandmother and step-grandfather, Florence and Roscoe, coming home one spring after spending the winter in Florida, brimming with enthusiasm about a new task, learning Spanish. A number of my relatives couldn't understand why they would undertake such a project. "What in the world do you want to try to learn Spanish for? You're almost 80 years old. You can't learn Spanish — it's too difficult."

The matter was a simple one for my grandparents. They needed to learn Spanish because they had been working as volunteers in Sarasota, driving people to the doctor's office, delivering meals, and running various errands. Many of the people they were helping did not speak English. Instead of saying, "We've got to teach these people English," they said, "We need to learn Spanish."

In response to our relatives saying, "Geez, you're too old. Why try to learn Spanish at your age?" my grandma replied, "Well, I certainly can't get any younger and I want to know it. There's no reason why I can't learn Spanish."

To say that she became fluent in a second language at that relatively late stage of her life would be an exaggeration, but she certainly did learn enough Spanish to be able to communicate with those migrant workers in Florida, and she was quite proud of her accomplishments, as I was, also.

I had many reasons to respect and admire my grandmother, and this episode added to the list. Her example reminds me that we are all capable — indeed, it is our duty, to learn something new every day.

> **"It's what you learn after you know it all that counts."** - John Wooden

It works well for me to equate mental stretching with physical stretching. If we fail to stretch on a regular basis, we become stiff. Mental rigor mortis (also called paradigm paralysis, or hardening of the attitudes) dooms us to vocational failure and, more importantly, a general outlook of unhappiness.

So, be on the lookout for new (and fun) ways to challenge your mental comfort zone on a regular basis.

PERSPECTIVE # 21

I Make and Take Time to Read

Learning to read and having the ability to read is one of the our most precious gifts. Yet somehow in this high-tech world, reading has become almost obsolete. For example, when someone asks, "Have you read the book?" the typical answer is, "I'll wait until the movie comes out."

Making time to read means that I include reading in my daily schedule. Taking time to read means that I don't resent spending that time reading. I exhibit my appreciation with a daily allotment of time set aside for this important activity.

I'd also like to recommend that you consider taking a reading course that will improve your speed and retention. An excuse for not reading that I have used for many years is the fact that I am a relatively poor reader. When I read, my thought process is nearly the same as when I'm speaking; I speak (and read) at a pace of about 125 to 150 words a minute, and that simply isn't fast enough to keep my conscious and subconscious mind occupied.

What often happens is that I get to the bottom of a page and wonder what I just read. I'll realize that I've been thinking about an upcoming appointment, an athletic event, or a future speaking engagement — my mind simply wasn't on what I was reading, and my retention was practically nil. I know that if I were a faster reader my retention would be better, and it would be easier to justify the time set aside to read.

> **"The person who does not read is no better off than the person who cannot read."**

I'm also a big proponent of listening to audio books or cassette tapes, particularly while I'm driving. Driving an automobile is basically a subconscious function, so I can concentrate on the material being discussed, and my retention from listening to materials on tape while driving is just incredible. It's got to be eight to ten times better than my retention from simply reading material. I'm not suggesting that tapes should replace books, but my personal experience has been that tapes can be a terrific supplement.

Another sticking point about reading is that too often people flip through the pages of a book and think, "My gosh, this is 350 pages long. It will take me forever to read it. I'll never finish it, so I may as well not even start."

For these people, I recommend starting a reading program that involves just 15 minutes a day. If you read 15 minutes a day, in an average month you'll spend seven and one-half hours reading. An average reader will be able to complete most books in that amount of time. By simply devoting 15 minutes per day to reading, you can read one book a month.

Try this one on for size: If I were to challenge you to read 60 books in the next five years, you might say, "Yeah, right, 60 books! Are you nuts? I could never read that much." Stop and think about it: 60 books in five years is only one book a month. To attain that goal you need only read 15 minutes each day.

A sage person once said, "The difference between who you are today and who you are two years from now, will be in the people you've met and the books you've read."

Please read. Make the time. Take the time. You don't have to become a bookworm to achieve some marvelous, if not miraculous, results.

PERSPECTIVE # 22

I Have a Good Awareness of Myself

When I think about having a good awareness of myself, what really comes to my mind is living in the *now*, being involved in what is presently going on, not worrying about either the past or the future. I choose to be aware of how my behavior is being affected by my emotional states and energy levels and how my moods and behaviors are affecting the moods and behaviors of people around me.

I work at having a clear understanding of the different factors that go into influencing who I am, what kind of mood I am in, and what level of energy I am experiencing. I need to be aware of those factors, along with my physical pains, my thought patterns, my paradigms, and my ingrown prejudices that are built on my experiences. Experience can be a good thing; experience can be a bad thing.

I once heard this example about experience being overrated: "A cat that has sat on a hot stove will never sit on a hot stove again. He has experience. But he will never sit on a cold stove either."

Possessing the judgment to apply experience makes all the difference. Being aware of my present moods, health, emotional states, and energy levels will help me decide whether now is a good time to make a decision, or if I should be more patient and a little less aggressive. There are times when I am calm and rational, neither depressed or hyped up, when I can trust my first judgment quite well. But there are other times when that is probably not going to be such a good idea.

An important indicator of unhealthy self-awareness is denial.

Denial of either the contributing factors and/or the end result
(disruptive/self-defeating behaviors) is undoubtedly the biggest and
most important hurdle that must be cleared before improvement may
be realized. It often is the stumbling block that prevents many
attempted programs from overcoming even the initial inertia.

> ## Denial is not just a big river in Egypt.

I have developed a skill that I would wager is a common one for
too many people: I now am able to precisely analyze and critique my
behavior — several hours later. Does the phrase "too little, too late"
pop into your mind?

The critical point is to be able to have that crucial awareness in
the present moment. Unfortunately, the following maxim is painfully
accurate: The times when we need it (self-awareness) the most, is when
we have it the least. When are these times? I'm glad you asked.
Clearly, we present the most danger to ourselves and to others when we
are operating under the dark cloud of the stress response.

When we experience anger, fear, frustration, anxiety, or that
lovely feeling of vengeance, we are most likely to lose our presence of
mind. Quick trip to the bottom line — we become more animal-like
(more on this in the next Perspective).

A powerful strategy is to identify symptomatic behaviors and
have responses prepared for them. Raising your voice, pounding your
fist, throwing a golf club, might all be subtle hints you could pick up on.

On a personal note, I tend to allow anxiety to sneak me in the back door of the stress response. The key behavior I'm on guard for is the deterioration of my vocabulary. Using words my wife describes as "talking like a pirate," is the indicator. Employing an appropriate stress-reducing tactic is the response.

I Maintain Control Over My Emotional States and Energy Levels

This Perspective is a direct reference to the theory of mental toughness, as it is outlined by Dr. James Loehr in his excellent book for athletes, *Mental Toughness Training for Sports*, and in a follow-up book, *Mentally Tough*, which applies the same principles to people in business. Maintaining control over emotional states and energy levels is in fact the definition of mental toughness, according to Dr. Loehr.

If you've ever heard me speak, chances are pretty good that you've seen me do the Mental Toughness lecture (it comprises about 40 percent of all my presentations). To shorten that information into a few paragraphs is a big order. Briefly, I would say that emotional state is a person's mood. Either mood or attitude would be a good substitute for emotional state. The use of the words "energy levels" is more common than "emotional states," and the interpretation is more straightforward.

Both emotional states and energy levels are very subjective matters. They cannot be measured or quantified, which makes it difficult to get a good handle on them. We need to understand how emotional states and energy levels affect our performance and how different combinations of these two factors form different variations of our own natural behavioral styles.

First, let's divide emotional states into good or bad, positive or negative. Next, divide energy levels into high or low. When you cross-reference these two conditions, each of which has two possible variables, you end up with four possible combinations of emotional states and energy levels: high energy coupled with positive emotional states; negative emotional states connected with high energy levels; low energy levels paired with negative emotional states; and finally, low energy levels and positive emotional states.

For short, let's call these four states High Positive, High Negative, Low Negative, and Low Positive. Each of the states acts as a behavior modifier and as such can be used to predict performance levels.

To begin with, we must understand where we are on the mental toughness matrix (the self-awareness we discussed in the previous affirmation). Then we have to know how the state we're presently in affects our ability to do whatever task is at hand.

Of the four states, High Negative evokes the most measurable, quantifiable response, almost a reflex action. This is called the fight-or-flight syndrome. Our species has somehow lowered the threshold of threat required to trigger this reflex from life-threatening to ego-threatening, hence the more contemporary reference to stress response.

There are a number of physical manifestations associated with stress response that affect us very negatively: increased blood pressure and pulse rate, excessive perspiration, quick and shallow breathing (causing poor oxygen supply to muscles and brain), accelerated rate of fatigue, digestive disruption, and a toxic focus to our judgement (just to name a few). While the thought that the stress response, or the fight-or-flight syndrome, helps our energy levels by giving us a shot of adrenaline has some truth to it, the downside of its effects wins in a landslide.

Now, part one of the Perspective — "emotional state control" —

starts with accepting complete responsibility for my emotions. I act, not react, and when I backslide and react, I perform damage control the moment my awareness kicks in (review previous Perspective).

The second half of this Perspective — energy level control — is a concept that might baffle most of us at first. I believe the most common perception is one that makes us passive recipients of our energy levels. When I ask an athlete, salesperson, business leader, etc., if they have an energy strategy, they look at me as though I'm from another planet.

Granted, some important influences on our energy levels may be temporarily out of our control — illness, injury, extreme weather, work, family demands, etc. However, take a long hard look at this list of significant factors concerning energy levels and then think about how much control we really do have over each one:

- What kind of shape are we in?
- How much do we weigh?
- What kinds of foods do we eat (and, when do we eat them)?
- How much sleep are we getting (and how much before midnight)?
- Are we participating in a regular exercise program?
- Do we partake of alcohol or drugs?

Far too many of us abdicate control of energy levels simply by failing to have a plan.

The entire concept of mental toughness requires a more detailed explanation than is possible for this particular Perspective, but I think you get the idea. The real value of this Perspective is to remind ourselves that we're in control of our emotional states and energy levels. We're not just a product of our environment; we're not just a product of our genetics. We have many choices, and we can have a great deal of control over these two vitally important factors. We must make certain we exercise intelligent use of that control.

> **"Mental toughness is essential to success."** - Vince Lombardi

I Am Focused on the *Now*

A study of different types of worries conducted by the University of Michigan several years ago reported that approximately 40 plus percent of the things people were worried about had already happened. Another 30 plus percent were never going to happen, and roughly 10 percent involved areas beyond the person's control. In total, 92.5 percent of everything that people reported being worried about involved items that had happened in the past, could happen in the future, or were areas over which they had no control.

We can't ignore the past. We must learn from the past, but we can't live there. We must prepare for the future, but we can't live in the future either, so we can't become overly concerned about it.

> **"I'm an old man now. In my life I've experienced many terrible things; a few of which actually happened."**
> - Samuel Clemens

The present is where we are right *now*. We have to make sure that we are doing our best *now*. Being focused on the *now* is simply a matter of living in the present, being part of what is happening and understanding how our presence and behavior is affecting the people around us.

Look around you (maybe you only have to go as far as a

mirror). Listen to the amount of conversation in our daily lives that is based on rehashing the past (over and over again), worrying about the future, or anticipating the splendor of life when some event finally occurs. The small amount of time we live in the present will astound you.

I believe we make three fundamental errors in thinking when we live in time periods other than the present:

1. The past is past, good or bad. The name of the species is human being, not human scrapbook. Get over it; get on with it; get INTO it.

2. The things we worry about rarely come to pass, and if they do, they are usually not as bad as anticipated, and if they are — the worrying didn't help anyway (and it probably contributed to our being less able to cope).

3. If we delay permission to be happy or satisfied until the destination is reached, we miss all the joy of the journey.

Just as important is the fact that when we dwell on the past, or future, or both, our concentration (and with it our performance) in the present suffers. This leads to a self-fulfilling prophecy of failure and self-defeating behaviors that hinder success.

All the "Wake-up and smell the coffee" (or whatever) jokes, really mean "Come back to reality." They are a rewrite of the classic phrase, "Take time to smell the roses," which is a reminder to appreciate more than just the visual beauty of that delicate (short-lived) flower. Being focused on the *now* is a terrific way to demonstrate gratitude for each and every moment of our lives.

I Am Upbeat and Energetic
Almost All the Time

As a professional speaker and staff trainer who emphasizes attitude, perspective, and personal control, I must walk my talk. I must demonstrate the things that I profess to other people as being positive and more productive ways of handling themselves.

I know that my mood, my personality style, and my way of conducting myself have a great influence over the people around me. We are not in this world alone. We are all part of a single, collective universal being. Our words, deeds, and thoughts *do* affect the people around us.

I also know that being upbeat and energetic describes being in the High Positive quadrant of the mental toughness matrix. This is the quadrant where the greatest productivity is accomplished, fewer errors are made, and health is also at its relative best.

Notice this Perspective says "almost all the time." I don't want to fall into the trap of thinking that this is the way I have to be every minute of every day. That would be an unrealistic expectation. In fact, it would not be a desirable goal because trying to stay in High Positive all the time leads to real burnout. To recuperate from strenuous efforts, we must allow the natural healing process to take place. For that to happen, we need to be peaceful, serene, and located in the low positive quadrant of the mental toughness matrix.

If this Perspective stated "every minute of the day" instead of "almost all the time," I would be setting up a guaranteed standard of failure. I could be upbeat and energetic 90 percent of the time and end up being focused on the failure of the other 10 percent. It's a poor idea. It's not realistic, and it's certainly not healthy.

We've already discussed the dangers of poor self-awareness. Without the awareness (the reminder) this Perspective provides, we can too easily slide into a state of attitude and energy levels that are only in response to our world, rather than a product/component of our master plan.

My choice is to have an attitude and style that is good for both me and for the people around me. Make special note of that word "choice." It implies a proactive decision. It means I have accepted the responsibility for determining my own level of mental toughness.

> **"It's always something."**
> - Gilda Radner

I Acknowledge Compliments With a Simple "Thank You"

This Perspective addresses a rather subtle problem that can evidence itself in people who aspire to be in the top five or ten percent of performers in any given discipline. What can happen, particularly if our upbringing has emphasized modesty, is that we brush off compliments with an "Aw, shucks, it was nothin'," kind of an attitude. On the surface, that may be seem to be modest and polite. But stop and think a moment: Someone is trying to pay you a compliment, and you are refusing to acknowledge it. (I can just see Miss Manners cringing now.)

When we refuse compliments or do not accept credit for an accomplishment, we are doing ourselves a major disservice. When we say, "Aw, shucks, it was nothin'," there are negative results: One is, the other person may begin to believe you. ("I guess it really wasn't a big deal; I shouldn't have gone out of my way to thank that person.") The other negative result is that you may begin to believe it yourself.

And, there's another level this unhealthy modesty can reach. Many of us take the concept of modesty, blow it out of proportion, and call it humor. Example: In response to a compliment about an athletic endeavor, a person might say, "Don't worry, I'll open my eyes next time."

I often stand in front of groups, stretch out my arms and say, "Standing in front of you today, ladies and gentlemen, is truly a world-class dieter. By that I mean that in my life I have lost hundreds of pounds. The problem is that I have gained back hundreds plus fifty." I usually get a chuckle out of that.

One of the things that I have recently discovered during these different periods of weight loss and weight gain, particularly during the losses, is that a number of people have been very kind to me and commented, "Say, Jerry, wow, it looks like you're losing some weight; it's looking good."

Being a modest, jovial kind of person, I have often replied, "Ha, ha, hey, don't worry, I'll find it again." That is intended to be a joke. Unfortunately, my body hasn't understood it as such and has turned it into a self-fulfilling prophecy.

Now, if someone says, "Jerry, it looks like you're losing weight," I look at them and simply say, "Thank you."

One way to accept a compliment if you are too modest to say, "Thank you, I'm proud of that," is to use the first person plural pronoun. Even if you are the only person who has participated in a certain project or activity, it's okay to say, "Thanks, we're proud of our efforts."

Often, when I'm joking around with my wife I'll respond to a compliment by saying, "Of course, dear, I am the best." Naturally, then she's sorry she ever paid me the compliment. But, the point of reinforcing the idea that I am of value, even when I'm just kidding around, is an important self-esteem, self-image type of thing.

When someone pays you a compliment, you should smile, nod, whatever, and just simply say, "Thank you." You do not have to go overboard with your appreciation, but don't turn it away either. It can make a big difference about how others think of you and an even bigger difference about how you view yourself.

Now remember, I started out this section by referring to aspirations of being an elite performer in a specific discipline. The sad truth is being a "top gun" and employing traditional modesty usually don't mix. Of course, exhibiting what I might refer to as traditional immodesty (being cocky, a braggart, etc.) will tend to lead to suffering by people around you and eventually to a lonely existence.

So where's the middle ground? It's simple. Being outwardly modest, while maintaining an inward abundance of confidence, will take you as far as you are capable of going.

> **When someone yells, "Great shot Jack", Nicklaus doesn't say, "It was just luck, I'll open my eyes next time." He looks them straight in the eye and says, "Thank you."**

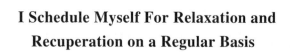

PERSPECTIVE # 27

I Schedule Myself For Relaxation and Recuperation on a Regular Basis

I think taking a break from your hectic schedule to recuperate and regain your edge is a lot like having children — if you wait until there's a good time to do it, it will never happen. You've just got to accept that it's a crucial concept and make it happen.

In today's world, we know that working hard is simply not good enough. We also need to work smart. Our efforts need to be as close to the point of peak productivity as possible. In order to accomplish that, we need to take time out on a regular basis so that when we are working, we obtain the maximum return on our efforts.

> **"For fast-acting relief,
> try slowing down."**
> - Lily Tomlin

The old model of vacationing for the successful person was spending a solid month or two in Florida, Palm Springs, Arizona, etc. In today's world — no way, it doesn't fit. An absence of that length of time would require a retraining program.

A more suitable vacation pattern for the successful person today might involve a three-day weekend every six weeks or so. Take a break; get chilled out, and come back ready to kick tail and take names.

On a short-term or daily basis, I employ a different philosophy.

Instead of shooting for rest and relaxation in segments of days, I try to be concerned about getting a regular workout. For me, that's restful, it is relaxation. It helps me keep sharp and working better.

A thought that often crosses my mind in very busy periods is, "Oh man, I've got so much stuff to do today, I can't even think about taking time for a workout." WRONG!

When those kinds of days pile up in a row, we end up not accomplishing much because we're functioning at such a low level of productivity. It's just not effective, it's a poor use of time.

I changed my former mind set to, "Whoa, I have a ton of things to do today. I can't afford to miss my workout." On a daily basis, I know I need my workouts to be my best. On a monthly or yearly basis, I know that I need to take regular breaks (two or three days) to stay sharp and work at peak levels.

I also know that I need to schedule those periods; I can't wait until it's convenient. If I wait on convenience, it will never come. My productivity will slow to a pace that is just not acceptable; my frustration will grow; I will gain weight; I will become agitated; my productivity will slip some more; the whole vicious cycle will get stronger and gain momentum.

Before you know it, the relationship with my family members is adversely affected, as well as my business relationships. The downward spiral of my life keeps gaining size and momentum. My life erodes in front of my very eyes. First I lose my business, then the motorcycle, then the boat, then the house, followed by my family — even the dog spurns me. WAIT A MINUTE! I don't even have a boat (nor do I want one); or a motorcycle (a Harley would be nice); or a dog (not while I live in the city). The point I'm trying to make (and in pretty dramatic fashion) is this: don't allow your box car to become attached to a runaway train like the one I've just described.

Do yourself a favor — do everybody in your life a favor — schedule yourself for regular R&R, and stick to that schedule.

PERSPECTIVE # 28

I Remain Calm, Relaxed and Pleasant
Under Trying Circumstances

This is a mind-set that was born for (and by) me.

This became a survival mechanism a number of years ago when I was going through a very bad situation.

As I look back on my life, I see my parents being divorced when I was 12, a nasty custody battle that took several years, my own marriage and divorce at a relatively young age, too many job changes, a number of grave and painful illnesses, and the deaths of several loved ones.

Yet, if I try to identify the most painful experience in my life, it was the bankruptcy that I experienced after my first attempt at starting my own company. I had a great concept for a company. It got off to a good start. I threw myself into this project, heart and soul. Along the way, I lost my perspective, did too many things to try to keep the business going, when I should have cut my losses and let it fold. I ended up losing a large amount of money, a great deal of it from several family members and friends.

Soon after, I was struggling big-time (as might be expected). It was all I could do to come up with interest payments for the money I owed. About one-third of the debt was owed to financial institutions, and I was making sporadic interest payments. Every time I sold off a piece of equipment from my company, I made payments. I was up front with them; they knew exactly what my situation was, but they just wouldn't leave me alone. They called me virtually every day. I stiff armed them for about a year, hoping that something would happen — my house would sell, I would win the lottery, somehow I would get my hands on enough cash to enable me to avoid the inevitable. Eventually I came to the realization I was going to have to file for bankruptcy. That was one of the hardest decisions of my life.

To make a bad situation worse, the banks to which I was in debt seemed to have collectively conspired to throw gas on my fire. I was getting daily telephone calls from several different institutions (the fact that I was not getting new information on a daily basis seemed to be lost on them). It got to the point that when the phone rang, I went ballistic. All it had to do was ring, and I was in a rage, I was defensive, I was aggressive, I started getting loud with these people, slamming down the phone. I thought of blowing a very loud whistle into the phone to get them to stop calling. It felt like blatant harassment, and I just couldn't understand it. I was not hiding, I was not trying to run away. Bankruptcy was the last thing on the face of the earth I wanted to do, but I felt as if they had backed me into a corner.

One of the many painful lessons I took away from that experience was that I was losing control. I was becoming excited, tense, and very unpleasant under the most trying circumstances that had ever existed in my life. I knew that I was not handling things well. I knew that had to change; I wanted to change. I wanted to be able to cope with the difficulties in my life to the best of my abilities.

Rather than be upset, tense and unpleasant, I decided I should try the opposite approach — being calm, relaxed, and pleasant.

The approach is simple, but it isn't easy. It was a good idea, but it took me a long time to integrate this behavior into my being and internalize the concept. I had great intentions, but I would often be surprised by something that would set me off. Minor gains seemed to take heroic efforts, only to be negated so easily by a setback.

I finally used visualization to help me accomplish the goal of this Perspective. I would picture myself being involved in a situation that could upset me. I would practice seeing myself on my internal video tape as being calm, feeling a smile come across my face, making sure I was breathing slowly and deeply and not feeling that inner tension that would start with my stomach and move out to my limbs and up into my chest — just being calm, relaxed and pleasant. I knew that this would not change the circumstances, but it would change my ability to handle them better.

The benefits were numerous. I simply felt better. I was more capable without those temporary blasts of insanity. I was certainly more fun (and much less frightening) to be around. Perhaps most importantly, regaining my self-control and pulling myself out of that increasingly downward spiral restored much of my shattered self-image.

What is your emotional Achilles' heel? Don't just try to cope. Turn it around. Get it over on the positive side of the ledger. It will feel great.

> **"If you make every game a life and death proposition, you're going to have problems. For one thing, you'll be dead a lot."** - Dean Smith

PERSPECTIVE # 29

I Marvel at Sunrises and Sunsets

Of all the concepts and little mind prods that I use, this is probably my favorite. I love the visual picture that this paints for me.

Sunrises and sunsets are truly one of our most beautiful, wonderful gifts, and we get them on a regular basis. Unfortunately, living here in Michigan, the continual cloud-cover reduces the number of horizontal masterpieces we are able to enjoy.

I use my response or reaction to a sunrise or a sunset as sort of a check and balance system for my mental health. If I see a beautiful sunrise or sunset, (and, frankly, I think they all are beautiful in varying degrees) and fail to stop, give thanks, let out a deep breath, and say, "Wow!" — then I know there's a good chance that something is wrong with me.

I am probably very preoccupied, quite possibly irritated, definitely not focused on the *now*. If I were, I would, indeed, be enjoying the natural beauty that was unfolding on the horizon.

I have a scenario that I enjoy playing out in my mind. I start by thinking of God as an entity recognizable in our world. Many people on our planet relate to God as a supreme being, or as a being far superior to us. Since we can't see Him, I choose to believe that He exists in a different dimension than we do. I think of God as being a superior being for our dimension. But in His dimension, He's just an average, common-folk-type person.

Like other people in His world, God would have decided on a career when he was just a very young supreme being. I like to think He grew up wanting to be an artist. That was His fervent wish; His heart's desire was to be an artist.

On our level, His creations are just incredible. But, in His dimension, His artistic talents were just so-so. He really didn't measure up to the competition, in terms of becoming a professional artist. So God decided He had to make a living some way, and so He went to a trade school (possibly Creator Tech) and became a creator. Upon graduation, He was given the project of creating this planet — Earth. "Here you go, God; here's some of the specifications of what we would like you to end up with; go ahead; make a run at it."

Imagine God at a social function in His world, and someone asks him, "So, what do you do?" and He says, "Well, I'm just a creator. I always wanted to be an artist, but I had to settle for being a creator."

We'd like to think He did a nice job, creating us in His image, all the incredible intricacies of our world and how they all fit together so well — He did a pretty decent job.

One nice thing about a creator's job is that you do most of your work in a fairly short period of time. Most of the rest of the time is spent observing, evaluating, and trying to lend help. So now that God has spare time, He indulges in His passion, which is art. He has many different art projects that He works on, but one of His favorites is sunrises and sunsets.

I like to view every sunrise and every sunset as a personally hand-created work of art from God, I take great comfort in that thought. I really enjoy watching a particularly spectacular array of colors and shapes. I like to smile and say to God, "Wow! Nice job. This one's really special. Interesting blend of colors. Love what you did with the clouds on this one."

I like to take a few moments and have a brief little chat with God and make certain I let Him know that somebody appreciates the incredible artist He is in our world.

When I do this, when I stop and take time to smell the roses (so to speak), when I appreciate the sunrises and sunsets, it's really impossible to suppress a smile. I get a nice, warm feeling all over (even in the dead of winter); I can almost feel my blood pressure go down. Then I know I am focused on the *now* — and I am in a good place.

"The sky is the daily bread of the eyes."
- Emerson

I Am At Peace With Myself.
I Like Me.

This last Perspective may seem odd, but it refers to an area of my life where I have particularly struggled. I often set incredibly high standards for myself and end up being only focused on my shortcomings. If I have a list of 20 things to do for the day and I complete 19, I have a tendency to beat myself up about the fact I didn't do number 20. This is unreasonable, counterproductive, and just generally a bad idea.

I also suffer from a common disease — woulda-coulda-shoulda thinking. We've already discussed this dangerous tendency: not being focused on the now, being focused on the things which haven't been accomplished rather than the things which have been.

I need to remind myself that I am really a nice fellow. My intentions are good; my organization just needs to be better (or maybe my expectations need to be a little more realistic). In fact, some of the traits that lead to my temporary setbacks are among the attributes that make me a neat person: my enthusiasm, my creativity, my intensity, my energy, etc. I need to cut myself some slack.

When I stop and think about it objectively, I really do deserve to be at peace with myself a little more often. When I pose the question, "Would I enjoy having a friend like me?" the answer is "Yes." It is not only appropriate, but important that I (and all of us) occasionally mouth the words, "I like me."

> **"I look back on my life like a good days work; it was done and now I'm satisfied with it."**
> - Grandma Moses

This final Perspective is probably the source for the title of this book. What good would it do you (or me) if we were successful with many of the other Perspectives and then spent time ruminating about the ones that needed work.

I recently met a most congenial fellow while I was sneaking out to the golf course on Key West during a business stay. As an aspiring golfer, I'm constantly searching for lightning to strike that special round where I break 80 or maybe shoot par for nine holes or something really memorable like that. Well, on this particular day, I was struggling big-time. Finally, after watching me hit some good shots, but also observing my frustration rising because I just wasn't scoring, this new golf partner looked at me calmly, smiled and said, "Jerry, not today." His words are still ringing in my ears. We can't be "on" all the time. Sometimes, we all just need to "LIGHTEN UP!"

You've already been more than polite by reading this much of the book, but I'm going to ask for one last indulgence. Please read aloud, "I like me." Again, please — like you mean it. "I like me." One last time, with feeling, "I LIKE ME."

Very good.

Thanks.

Epilogue

(Roscoe's passing)

Roscoe Witchell was my step-grandfather for 22 years. How he came to be my step-grandfather, (married to my paternal grandmother), is in itself a unique and heartwarming story that I promise to share with you at a future time.

Roscoe came into my life when I was a young boy, about eight years old. I was not only his step-grandson, I was his neighbor. We spent a great deal of time together for the following six or eight years. Roscoe was a large, lean, hardworking man who never left a doubt about where he stood on any issue, what he thought was right or wrong. Because of his openness and the time of my life that I was in contact with him, he had a great influence on me.

He believed in doing things the right way — period. He had been a carpenter for General Motors until his retirement. When it came time for us to tear down one of the old buildings on the farm — whether it was a granary, chicken coop, or whatever — that building came down just the way it went up, one nail at a time, one board at a time, one wall at a time. I learned more about construction and carpentry from that man by dismantling buildings than you can possibly imagine.

He also showed me, through the example of his life, the value of family and the importance they should be given. One of my most vivid recollections and contacts with Roscoe came on the evening of what would have been the biggest ballgame of my life to that point. I was about 12 years old. We were at the end of the season, playing for the Little League championship. We were playing the local rival. It was a classic "big game."

Throughout the season, I had played first base or third base. Now, due to the illness of another player, I was required to play short-stop. I was very nervous. At that time, Roscoe and my grandmother were the people in charge of my transportation. They had watched my games all season long and had followed the team closely.

It was a very tight game. The coach (who was my uncle) knew the game would be low-scoring. We were using a strategy of just trying to get one run at a time. When I came up to bat, the coach's strategy was to move the runner into scoring position. He asked me if I would bat left-handed to try to pull the ball to the right side of the infield. I had done this a number of times in practice, but never in a game situation. I agreed. I went to the plate, left-handed — and struck out. This was hard on me. I was used to experiencing a lot of success on the athletic field. I didn't like it. My next time up we had the same situation. Again, the coach wanted the runner moved to second base. This time, I approached him and said, "I can do that batting right-handed." Again, I struck out. This was very painful. Of the literally thousands of ballgames I've played before and after, that was the only time I've ever struck out twice in the same game. I was very distressed.

As the game went on, my team held a one-run lead going into the final inning. In their at-bat, the opposing team managed to load the bases with two outs: If we retire the batter, we win; if he gets a hit, at best the game is tied and we could possibly lose. The fate of both teams' seasons hinged on this batter. He hit a linedrive that went over the pitcher's head toward centerfield. I raced behind second base, my arm extended, and somehow, the ball hit my glove and stuck in the webbing. I stumbled, rolled and came up with the ball still in my glove. The batter was out! We won the game. We won the championship. The team was pumped.

As we drove away from the ballpark, I sat in the backseat of the car and began to cry. Roscoe realized I was crying. He turned around and said, rather gruffly, "What is wrong with you?" I sobbed back, "I can't believe I struck out twice." He slammed on the brakes, jumped out of the car, ran around to the door and pulled me out. "What in the world is wrong with you?" he screamed. "You just made a helluva play to win the game for your team. I'm very disappointed in you. You are more concerned with your personal accomplishments than you are with the success of the team. You'll never be a good ballplayer if you don't think more of the team than you do of your own individual statistics. I thought you were a better ballplayer than that."

His words still ring in my ears, 30 years later. I had a long and successful athletic career that revolved around a "team first" style of play.

The years passed, and Roscoe and my grandmother grew older. Roscoe had a stroke. He lost his ability to speak, and the rest of his health began to fail. It was obvious that as his speech and health left him, so did his desire to live. Although he couldn't express himself verbally, his frustrations became obvious. It became painful for me to visit my grandmother and Roscoe. My grandmother was going blind. Roscoe was miserable. His health deteriorated to the point where my grandmother could no longer care for him. He was moved into a nursing home.

Occasionally, I took my grandmother to the nursing home to visit Roscoe. How I hated that place. The smell of urine, the sight of older people struggling to maintain their equilibrium and their dignity. I remember the last time I saw Roscoe. I stood in the doorway of his room, looking at the naked, 85-pound skeleton of a man. The sight of him upset my grandmother tremendously. He didn't recognize either one of us. I never went back there again.

Several months later, the call came. Roscoe had finally passed on to a better place. I thought I was prepared for that moment, but I wasn't. The pain, the feeling of loss, the grief was tremendous. The funeral was held at the little country church where he and my grandmother had worshipped and had taken me and my sister so many times as children. I remember sitting in the last pew long after the service was over and wondering out loud, "Is that all there is?"

Roscoe was one of the most incredible people I had ever known. Now he was gone. How would the world ever come to understand the wonderful impact he had on me? The thought immediately crossed my mind that it sure as hell wouldn't happen by observing the way I was living my life. You see, I had heard Roscoe, I had watched him, but I hadn't allowed any of the lessons to sink in. The things he stood for had nothing to do with the way I was living my life. I knew that was wrong.

Soon after, I changed careers and "settled down." My wife and I eventually started a family. One of my greatest regrets in life is that I didn't straighten my life around while Roscoe was still living. I would have loved to show him by the example of my life that I had been paying attention.

I believe the greatest compliment we can pay a person is to lead our life according to the example they have provided.

Awareness is the first, crucial step. A decision to change/improve must be made; a plan of action devised. The outcome will hinge primarily on our follow-through. Poor follow-through of a great plan will net poor results.

This text was produced to help create an abundance of awareness. The impact of this important information is entirely up to you.

Decide.

Plan (get help if you need it).

Act.

The longer you wait, the more the spectrum of your choices will narrow.

A final acknowledgment:

Dear Roscoe,

I hope you're peering over our collective shoulders and that this text, this message, brings a smile to your soul.

Eternally grateful,

Jerry

An Open Invitation for Collaboration

So, if you're not doing anything pressing at the moment, "Wanna help me write a book?"

About halfway through this work, I started thinking about *Gaining MORE Essential Perspectives.* You've been reading about some "thought pattern changers" that have worked for me and, I hope, can work for you. Maybe a more important by-product of reading this book is that you will develop the understanding and the ability to create your own life-altering perspectives or "mini-mission statements" (as I like to call them).

If you have called upon short, affirmative phrases in the past that have been helpful in accomplishing positive, lasting changes in your life, there is an excellent chance those words could provide help for others, also. I'm planning on compiling the words and thoughts from all of you who choose to share your success stories with the rest of us into the next volume of this "series."

If you think that someone else might benefit from your insight, you're probably right. "If in doubt, send it out!" Please submit materials for consideration to:

The Harte Performance Group

P.O. Box 144

St. Johns, Michigan, 48879

Questions or comments? Call 1-800-562-5779.

I look forward to hearing from you. Be well. Play BIG!